Age Is Nothing but a State of Mind

ISBN: 978-1-59842-905-3

Wonderful Wacky Women®

Inspiring•Uplifting•Empowering

is a trademark of Suzy and Al Toronto. Used under license.

▐▌ and Blue Mountain Press are registered in U.S. Patent and Trademark Office. Certain trademarks are used under license.

Printed in China.
Second Printing: 2016

✪ This book is printed on recycled paper.

This book is printed on paper that has been specially produced to be acid free (neutral pH) and contains no groundwood or unbleached pulp. It conforms with the requirements of the American National Standards Institute, Inc., so as to ensure that this book will last and be enjoyed by future generations.

Blue Mountain Arts, Inc.
P.O. Box 4549, Boulder, Colorado 80306

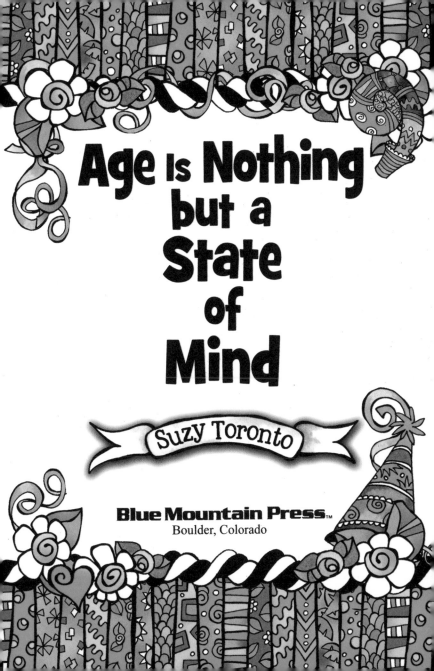

Age Is Nothing but a State of Mind

Suzy Toronto

Blue Mountain Press™
Boulder, Colorado

How old are you?
Personally, at this moment,
I have no idea how old I am.
I do remember a few
milestone birthdays,
you know, 18, 21, 40…
But in my head,
nothing has ever changed.
I keep wondering when
everyone is going to catch on
to the fact that for the last thirty years
I've been masquerading as an adult.

Perhaps we are, like the old saying goes,
"only as old as we feel."
In that case, I'll stay lost
in my bewilderment…
because really, life is what we make it
and age is nothing
but a state of mind.

© Suzy Toronto

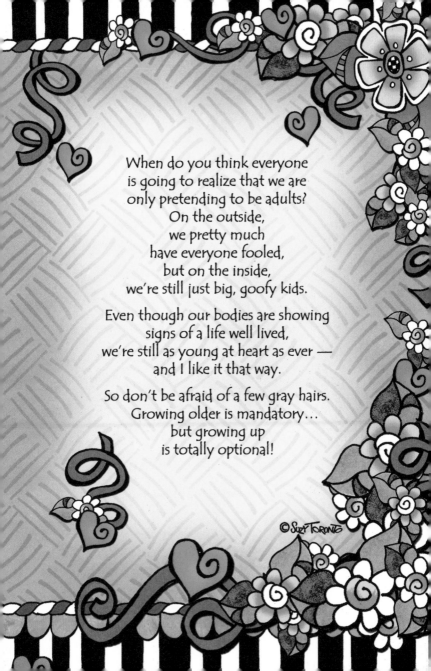

When do you think everyone
is going to realize that we are
only pretending to be adults?
On the outside,
we pretty much
have everyone fooled,
but on the inside,
we're still just big, goofy kids.

Even though our bodies are showing
signs of a life well lived,
we're still as young at heart as ever —
and I like it that way.

So don't be afraid of a few gray hairs.
Growing older is mandatory...
but growing up
is totally optional!

© Suzy Toronto

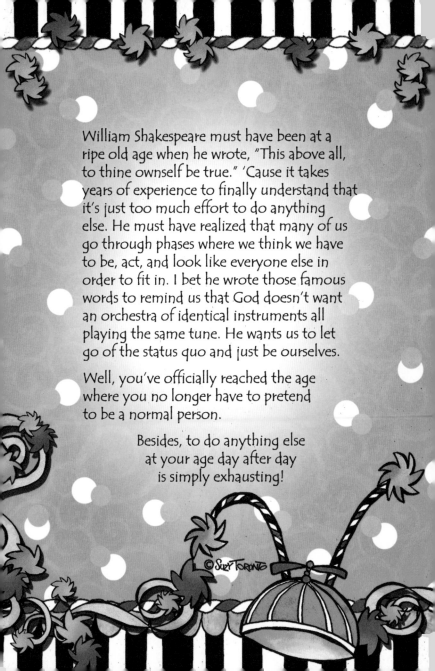

William Shakespeare must have been at a ripe old age when he wrote, "This above all, to thine ownself be true." 'Cause it takes years of experience to finally understand that it's just too much effort to do anything else. He must have realized that many of us go through phases where we think we have to be, act, and look like everyone else in order to fit in. I bet he wrote those famous words to remind us that God doesn't want an orchestra of identical instruments all playing the same tune. He wants us to let go of the status quo and just be ourselves.

Well, you've officially reached the age where you no longer have to pretend to be a normal person.

Besides, to do anything else
at your age day after day
is simply exhausting!

© Suzy Toronto

You Are
the Architect
of Your Own
Destiny

Acting fun and wacky
is the best part about
growing older.
Life's later years
are also
a great time to
let go of old ways
and choose to
embrace new paths
and unexplored
adventures.

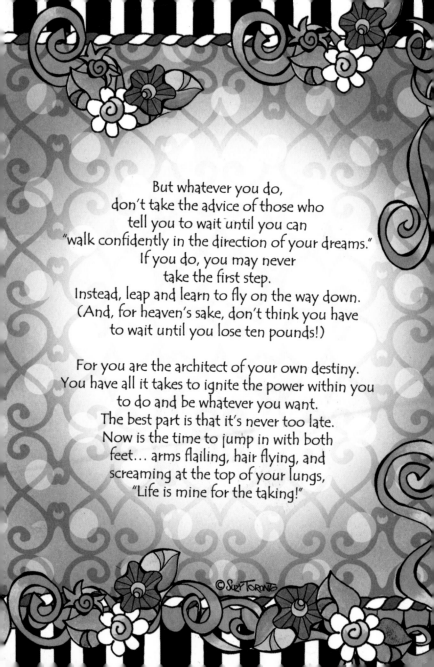

But whatever you do,
don't take the advice of those who
tell you to wait until you can
"walk confidently in the direction of your dreams."
If you do, you may never
take the first step.
Instead, leap and learn to fly on the way down.
(And, for heaven's sake, don't think you have
to wait until you lose ten pounds!)

For you are the architect of your own destiny.
You have all it takes to ignite the power within you
to do and be whatever you want.
The best part is that it's never too late.
Now is the time to jump in with both
feet... arms flailing, hair flying, and
screaming at the top of your lungs,
"Life is mine for the taking!"

© Suzy Toronto

Make Each Day Ridiculously Amazing

I believe with all my heart
that if I want to have an incredible day,
it's my responsibility to make it happen.
I need to convince myself that
no matter what stands in my way,
I am going to make it
ridiculously amazing.

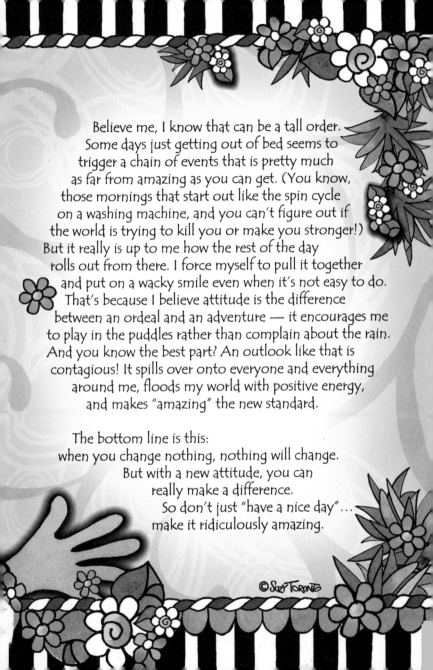

Believe me, I know that can be a tall order.
Some days just getting out of bed seems to
trigger a chain of events that is pretty much
as far from amazing as you can get. (You know,
those mornings that start out like the spin cycle
on a washing machine, and you can't figure out if
the world is trying to kill you or make you stronger!)
But it really is up to me how the rest of the day
rolls out from there. I force myself to pull it together
and put on a wacky smile even when it's not easy to do.
That's because I believe attitude is the difference
between an ordeal and an adventure — it encourages me
to play in the puddles rather than complain about the rain.
And you know the best part? An outlook like that is
contagious! It spills over onto everyone and everything
around me, floods my world with positive energy,
and makes "amazing" the new standard.

The bottom line is this:
when you change nothing, nothing will change.
But with a new attitude, you can
really make a difference.
So don't just "have a nice day"...
make it ridiculously amazing.

© Suzy Toronto

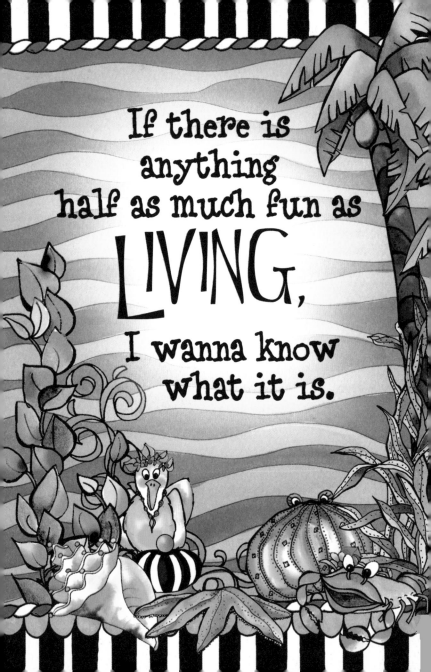

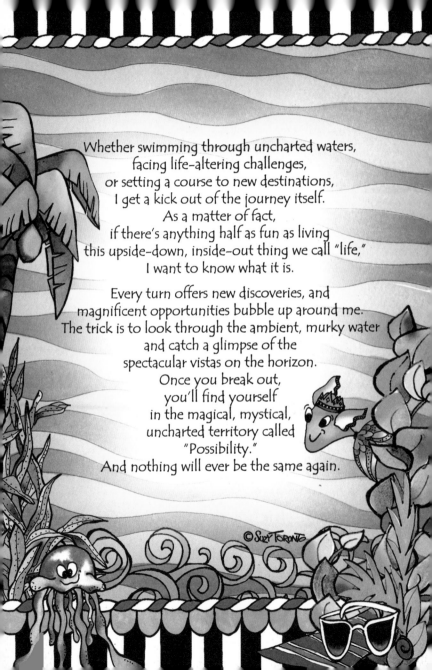

Whether swimming through uncharted waters,
facing life-altering challenges,
or setting a course to new destinations,
I get a kick out of the journey itself.
As a matter of fact,
if there's anything half as fun as living
this upside-down, inside-out thing we call "life,"
I want to know what it is.

Every turn offers new discoveries, and
magnificent opportunities bubble up around me.
The trick is to look through the ambient, murky water
and catch a glimpse of the
spectacular vistas on the horizon.
Once you break out,
you'll find yourself
in the magical, mystical,
uncharted territory called
"Possibility."
And nothing will ever be the same again.

© Suzy Toronto

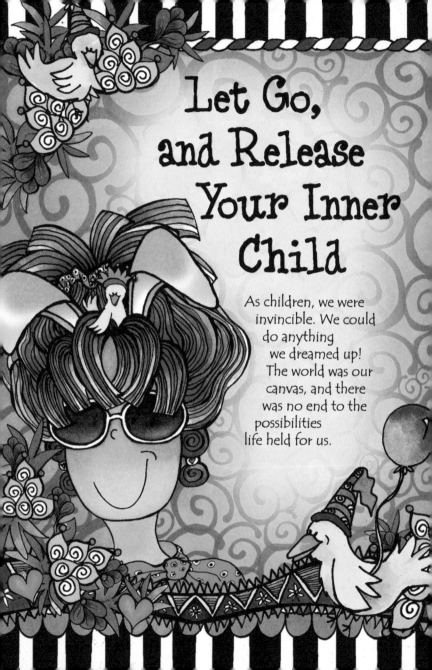

Let Go, and Release Your Inner Child

As children, we were invincible. We could do anything we dreamed up! The world was our canvas, and there was no end to the possibilities life held for us.

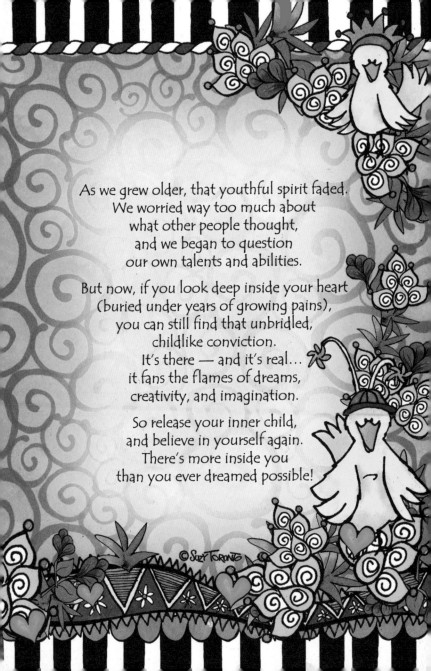

As we grew older, that youthful spirit faded.
We worried way too much about
what other people thought,
and we began to question
our own talents and abilities.

But now, if you look deep inside your heart
(buried under years of growing pains),
you can still find that unbridled,
childlike conviction.
It's there — and it's real...
it fans the flames of dreams,
creativity, and imagination.

So release your inner child,
and believe in yourself again.
There's more inside you
than you ever dreamed possible!

© Suzy Toronto

In our effort to masquerade as people who really have our acts together, goofs, blunders, and faux pas often slip out. Sometimes these missteps are so unforgettable that they start to take on a life of their own. We get our feet stuck so far in our mouths or our skirts flung up so high over our heads that the spectacle is simply hard to miss.

This is where laughing at ourselves becomes a lifesaving virtue… because when we embrace our mistakes and make the best of the situation, we can just move on. After all, if there is going to be a big, goofy elephant in the room, you might as well introduce her!

So next time your
    inner "goofball" slips out,
        muster up all the wild energy
            you possess,
        throw your arms in the air,
    and give the world
a cross-eyed smile!

After all, we may do
    foolish things…
        but at least we do them
            with enthusiasm!

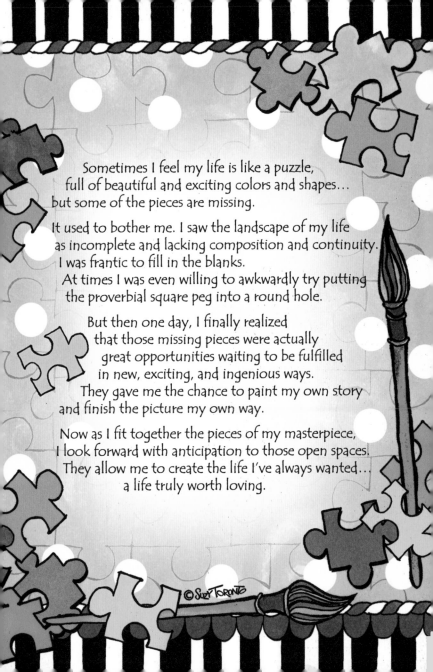

Sometimes I feel my life is like a puzzle,
full of beautiful and exciting colors and shapes...
but some of the pieces are missing.

It used to bother me. I saw the landscape of my life
as incomplete and lacking composition and continuity.
I was frantic to fill in the blanks.
At times I was even willing to awkwardly try putting
the proverbial square peg into a round hole.

But then one day, I finally realized
that those missing pieces were actually
great opportunities waiting to be fulfilled
in new, exciting, and ingenious ways.
They gave me the chance to paint my own story
and finish the picture my own way.

Now as I fit together the pieces of my masterpiece,
I look forward with anticipation to those open spaces.
They allow me to create the life I've always wanted...
a life truly worth loving.

©Suzy Toronto

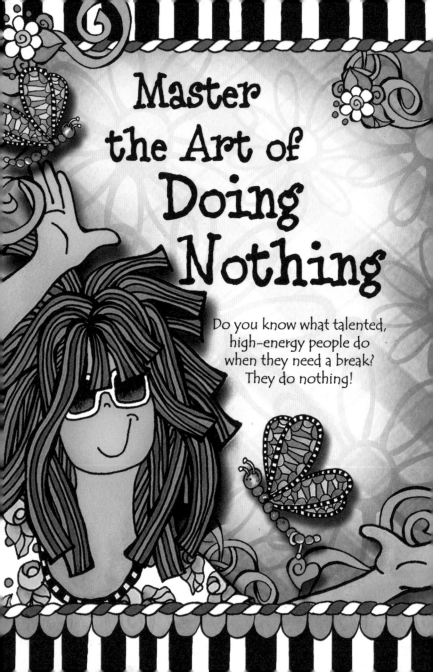

Master the Art of Doing Nothing

Do you know what talented, high-energy people do when they need a break? They do nothing!

I'm not saying they don't take time off
or go on vacation…
they most certainly do!
But instead of running around
at 90 mph
trying to do and see everything,
they concentrate on
not doing anything at all.

It's not about being lazy.
It's about taking the time to breathe…
zoning out to zero for a few days
and stepping back from normal life to regroup.

It takes years to master, but once you perfect it,
you'll realize how wonderful it is.
With both body and spirit renewed,
you'll agree it is time well spent.
So give "doing nothing" a try.
I think you're going to be really great at it!

©Suzy Toronto

Becoming an Adult Is the Dumbest Thing I Ever Did

Like most young people, I couldn't wait to come of age, become free to make my own choices and decisions about my life, and be a real, certified grownup. I wanted, wished, and waited with anticipation for my birthday so I could declare to the world that I was officially an adult. But you know what? Becoming an adult is the dumbest thing I ever did.

Now I wonder why I was in such a hurry. Why did I think being responsible for everyone and everything in the known universe was something I needed to do? Why did I think that leaving behind the carefree days of my youth in exchange for having to act like an adult was going to be so fabulous?

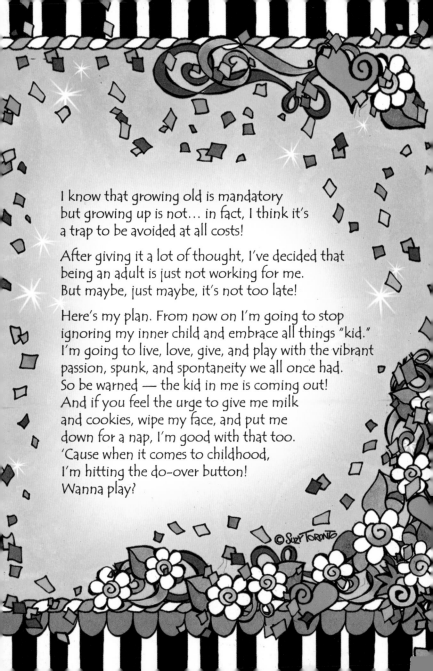

I know that growing old is mandatory
but growing up is not… in fact, I think it's
a trap to be avoided at all costs!

After giving it a lot of thought, I've decided that
being an adult is just not working for me.
But maybe, just maybe, it's not too late!

Here's my plan. From now on I'm going to stop
ignoring my inner child and embrace all things "kid."
I'm going to live, love, give, and play with the vibrant
passion, spunk, and spontaneity we all once had.
So be warned — the kid in me is coming out!
And if you feel the urge to give me milk
and cookies, wipe my face, and put me
down for a nap, I'm good with that too.
'Cause when it comes to childhood,
I'm hitting the do-over button!
Wanna play?

©Suzy Toronto

Seek Always the True Treasures of Life

Life can get confusing.
Sometimes we mix up our priorities
so much that we end up in
uncharted waters seeking
the lost treasures of the world.
We find ourselves drifting into
currents that carry us away
to artificial vistas
masked in glitz
and baubles.

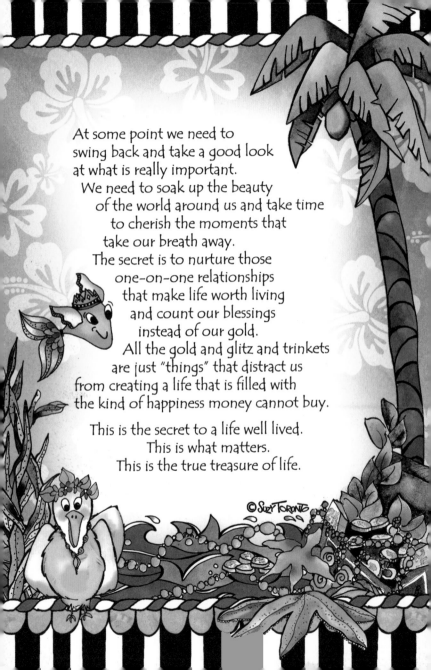

At some point we need to
swing back and take a good look
at what is really important.
We need to soak up the beauty
of the world around us and take time
to cherish the moments that
take our breath away.
The secret is to nurture those
one-on-one relationships
that make life worth living
and count our blessings
instead of our gold.
All the gold and glitz and trinkets
are just "things" that distract us
from creating a life that is filled with
the kind of happiness money cannot buy.

This is the secret to a life well lived.
This is what matters.
This is the true treasure of life.

©Suzy Toronto

Life Is Short...
Go for the
Cupcakes!

Being a practical person is a good thing.
In a world of crippling debt,
overindulgence,
and instant gratification,
tightening your belt a bit
is wise and prudent.
But extremes in either
direction are not the answer.
Self-deprivation can be
just as damaging as
going the opposite way,
to the point where
we lose our
appetite to grow,
experience,
and enjoy life.

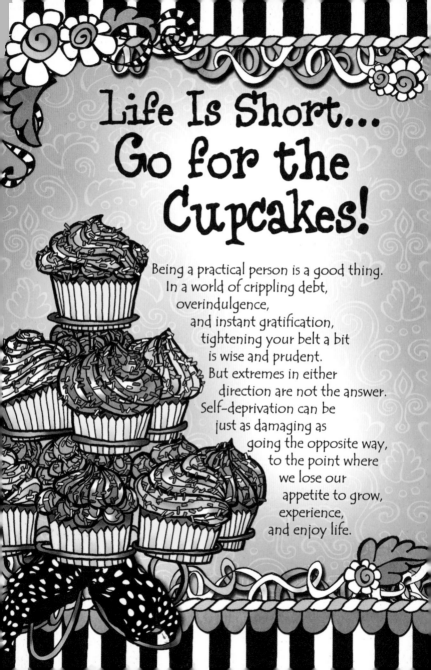

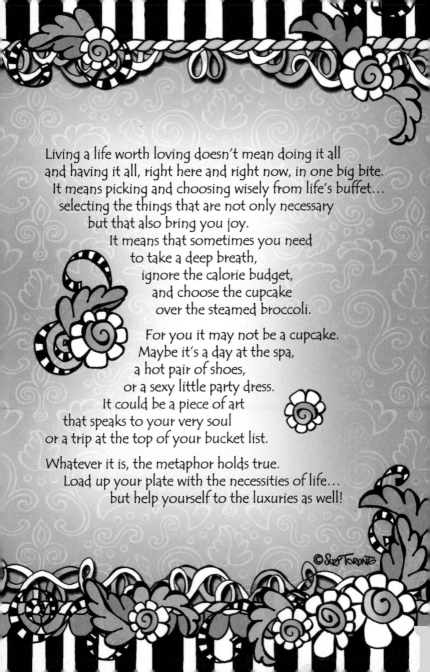

Living a life worth loving doesn't mean doing it all
and having it all, right here and right now, in one big bite.
It means picking and choosing wisely from life's buffet…
selecting the things that are not only necessary
but that also bring you joy.
It means that sometimes you need
to take a deep breath,
ignore the calorie budget,
and choose the cupcake
over the steamed broccoli.

For you it may not be a cupcake.
Maybe it's a day at the spa,
a hot pair of shoes,
or a sexy little party dress.
It could be a piece of art
that speaks to your very soul
or a trip at the top of your bucket list.

Whatever it is, the metaphor holds true.
Load up your plate with the necessities of life…
but help yourself to the luxuries as well!

© Suzy Toronto

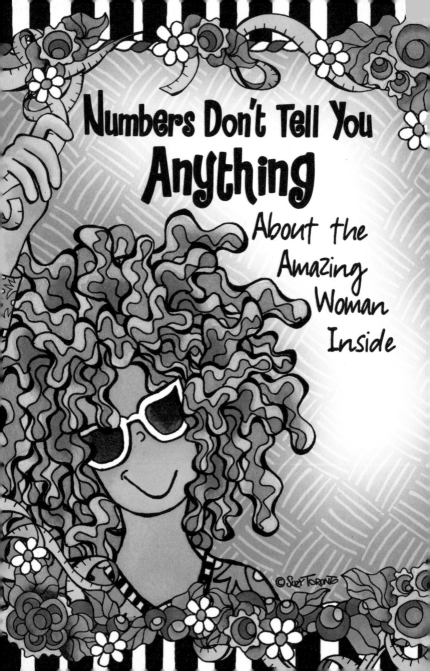

As women, we are often analyzed in a myriad
of different ways to see if we measure up.
    We are judged to be too big or too small,
too round, too straight, too tall, too short.
We are compared against numbers
    like 36-24-36… in inches, in sizes, and in age —
all things that shouldn't matter.

If we are to be measured as women,
    let it be by the things that really count —
        the depth of our compassion,
        our thirst for knowledge,
            and our tremendous grace under fire.
        Let the breadth of our integrity
            and the width of our honor
            be more accurate measures
            of who we truly are
            rather than the size of our jeans
            or the date of our birth.

        Because in the end, all the inches and ages
            and sizes are just numbers…
                and numbers don't tell you anything
                about the amazing woman inside!

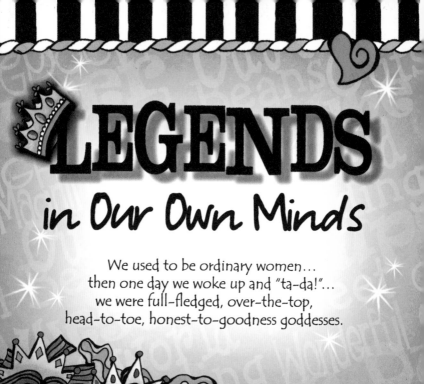

LEGENDS
in Our Own Minds

We used to be ordinary women…
then one day we woke up and "ta-da!"…
we were full-fledged, over-the-top,
head-to-toe, honest-to-goodness goddesses.

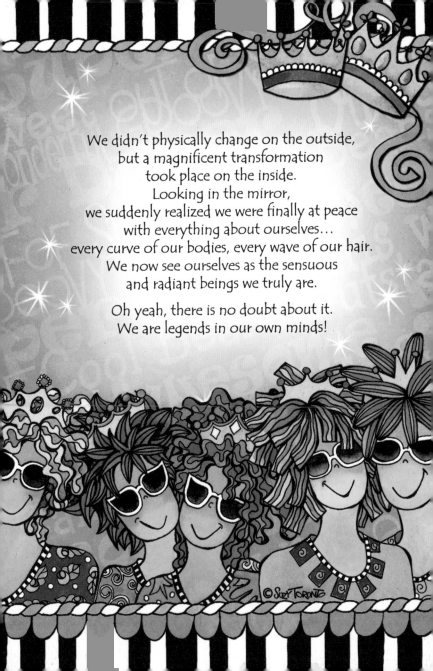

We didn't physically change on the outside,
but a magnificent transformation
took place on the inside.
Looking in the mirror,
we suddenly realized we were finally at peace
with everything about ourselves…
every curve of our bodies, every wave of our hair.
We now see ourselves as the sensuous
and radiant beings we truly are.

Oh yeah, there is no doubt about it.
We are legends in our own minds!

© Suzy Toronto

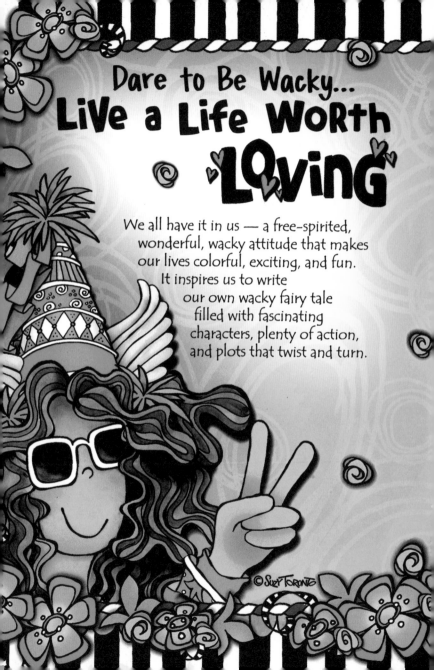

Dare to Be Wacky...
LiVe a Life WORth
LOvinG

We all have it in us — a free-spirited,
wonderful, wacky attitude that makes
our lives colorful, exciting, and fun.
It inspires us to write
our own wacky fairy tale
filled with fascinating
characters, plenty of action,
and plots that twist and turn.

© Suzy Toronto

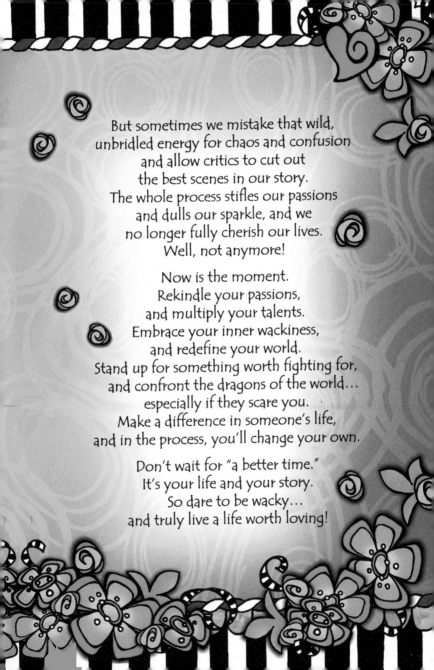

But sometimes we mistake that wild,
unbridled energy for chaos and confusion
and allow critics to cut out
the best scenes in our story.
The whole process stifles our passions
and dulls our sparkle, and we
no longer fully cherish our lives.
Well, not anymore!

Now is the moment.
Rekindle your passions,
and multiply your talents.
Embrace your inner wackiness,
and redefine your world.
Stand up for something worth fighting for,
and confront the dragons of the world...
especially if they scare you.
Make a difference in someone's life,
and in the process, you'll change your own.

Don't wait for "a better time."
It's your life and your story.
So dare to be wacky...
and truly live a life worth loving!

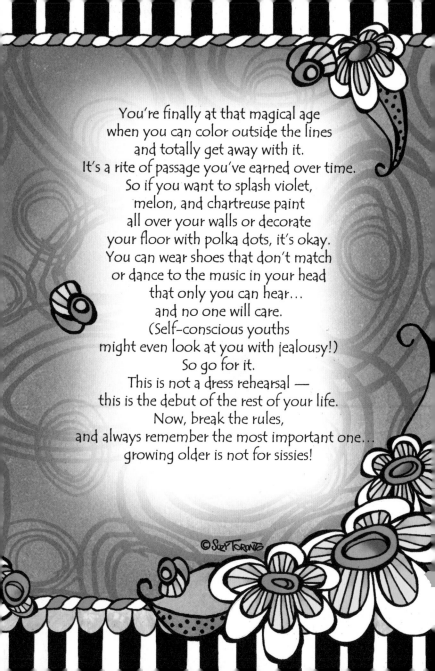

You're finally at that magical age
when you can color outside the lines
and totally get away with it.
It's a rite of passage you've earned over time.
So if you want to splash violet,
melon, and chartreuse paint
all over your walls or decorate
your floor with polka dots, it's okay.
You can wear shoes that don't match
or dance to the music in your head
that only you can hear…
and no one will care.
(Self-conscious youths
might even look at you with jealousy!)
So go for it.
This is not a dress rehearsal —
this is the debut of the rest of your life.
Now, break the rules,
and always remember the most important one…
growing older is not for sissies!

© Suzy Toronto

Wonderful Wacky Words
to Make Your
Heart Tingle

Life is too short to wear pantyhose 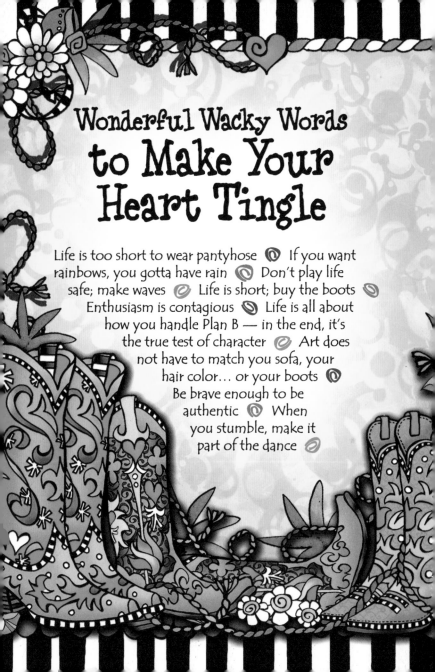 If you want rainbows, you gotta have rain Don't play life safe; make waves Life is short; buy the boots Enthusiasm is contagious Life is all about how you handle Plan B — in the end, it's the true test of character Art does not have to match you sofa, your hair color… or your boots Be brave enough to be authentic When you stumble, make it part of the dance

Always color outside the lines  Play with wild abandon When taking the road less traveled, it's best to wear a rockin' hot pair of boots Happiness is always an inside job When life gets crazy, do something normal… and if life gets too normal, do something crazy No one's last words were ever "I wish I'd eaten more celery sticks" When life gets stormy, pull on your boots and go look for puddles to play in Dream with your eyes wide open And the most important thing to know… age is nothing but a state of mind. So pick an age you like, and stick to it!

© Suzy Toronto

About the Author

So this is me... I'm a tad wacky and just shy of crazy. I'm fiftysomething and live in the sleepy village of Tangerine, Florida, with my husband, Al, and a big, goofy dog named Lucy. And because life wasn't crazy enough, my eightysomething-year-old parents live with us too. (In my home, the nuts don't fall far from the tree!) I eat far too much chocolate, and I drink sparkling water by the gallon. I practice yoga, ride a little red scooter, and go to the beach every chance I get. I have five grown children and over a dozen grandkids who love me as much as I adore them. I teach them to dip their French fries in their chocolate shakes and to make up any old words to the tunes they like. But most of all, I teach them to never, ever color inside the lines. This is the Wild Wacky Wonderful life I lead, and I wouldn't have it any other way. Welcome to my world!